D1083880

PETE AND PENNY
KNOW AND
GROW

PETE AND PENNY KNOW AND GROW

*Devotional Readings for Boys and Girls
Five to Nine Years Old*

by

DOROTHY GRUNBOCK JOHNSTON

MOODY PRESS • CHICAGO

Printed in the United States of America

Contents

5

Introduction

This is the second book in the Pete and Penny series. The first, *Pete and Penny Play and Pray,* already has reached around the world, making Pete and Penny as personal as first cousins to many families.

Pete and Penny Know and Grow is for use by boys and girls who have reached the age where the habit of personal devotions can be developed. Ideally, this habit starts within the family circle, when the entire family together has a plan of daily devotions.

While the Bible is *the* Book on which family devotions are based, other books should also be selected which center around the Word of God and show applications of its teachings. Both Pete and Penny books have this purpose. Each is written as a continuous story, featuring the experiences of a family and especially focusing on the activities of Pete and Penny, eight-year-old twins. Each chapter is an episode for a daily reading. The book might be read for a week or several days and alternated with Bible readings. Or scripture passages used in the Pete and

Penny stories may be read again from a modern translation, such as the *Living Bible,* the New American Standard Bible, or Williams's New Testament, and discussed further in the family circle. Perhaps the Pete and Penny book may be turned over to the child for his own devotional reading.

Every daily episode presents a story in which arises a life problem common to children. Pete and Penny are typical children who have the normal reactions to temptations, rules and regulations, living together, and influences from their friends. For instance, they must learn not to cheat at school nor to grumble about doing chores nor to be vain about achievements. Mother and Daddy are perhaps ideal parents who are able to introduce patiently the Bible instruction needed for each problem situation. Appropriate Scripture is read, the application is seen, and Pete and Penny—out of a desire to please God—learn to respond correctly.

It is the author's plan and hope that these episodes of Pete and Penny inspire young readers also to develop mature Christian attitudes.

A New House for the Pendletons

PETE AND PENNY found Daddy and Mother sitting at the kitchen table.

"Do you like this one or that one?" asked Daddy.

Mother looked at the magazine. Finally, she said, "This would fit our family the best."

Penny peeked over Mother's shoulder. She had her finger on the picture of a house with a house plan beside it.

Penny was curious. "Tell me, Mother, what would fit our family?"

"This house, Penny. The house we live in is too small for us now, and God is helping Daddy earn enough money; so I think He would be pleased if we had a new house."

"Pete! Did you hear? A new house!" Penny danced up and down.

Soon Daddy paid for a lot on the edge of town. It was a whole acre of woods. What excitement there was in the Pendleton house the day the bulldozer was to come! They were all up early and ate their breakfast in a hurry so that they could drive over and see the digging. Trees were being cleared away.

9

Pete and Penny stood back where they could not be hurt.

The man climbed up a tall tree and hooked a cable around it. The other end of the cable was fastened to the tractor.

As soon as the man was down, the big bulldozer started to chug and choke and puff and sputter. The tall tree leaned and then toppled over with a crash!

"Boy," said Pete, "that was fun! I want to be a bulldozer man when I grow up."

With its big blade, the bulldozer pushed the tree over to a pile. Tree after tree went toppling to the ground. Pete and Penny watched every one.

The new lot wasn't far from their old house. Mother decided to drive home and fix a picnic lunch.

"May we go?" asked Pete. "We want to invite Bob and Janey to come back. They would love to watch, too."

"Yes," said Penny, "the big blade will start to dig the dirt after lunch. They can eat a picnic lunch with us and then watch."

A few minutes later, Pete and Penny jumped out of the car and dashed toward the Barbers' house.

Janey and Bob were husking corn on the back porch steps.

"We are going to have a new house," puffed Pete.

11

"Come have a picnic lunch with us. It's fun to watch the bulldozer."

"No thanks," said Janey with a sneer in her voice. "We sure are glad to hear you are going to move. The quicker the better. And we don't want to watch your old bulldozer, do we Bob?"

Bob just husked corn.

"There is the gate," said Janey. "You look better on the other side."

Pete and Penny felt sad and confused. Janey and Bob were being mean to them again, even though they had said they wanted to be friends.

Back home, Pete moaned. "I showed love, Mother. I gave her the dish garden and she is still mean."

"Longsuffering is one very necessary fruit of the Spirit," Mother told them. "You may have to be patient and kind for a long time." Then she opened Daddy's big Bible and read:

> Walk worthy of the Lord unto all pleasing, being fruitful in every good work, and increasing in the knowledge of God; strengthened with all might, according to his glorious power, unto all patience and longsuffering with joyfulness (Colossians 1:10-11).

"It's hard to suffer for a long time and be happy about it," Pete said.

"With God's help, you can," replied Mother.

Tunnels and Houses out of Dirt

THE BIG TREES that had been pushed down by the bulldozer at the lot had to be trimmed. Daddy lopped off branches with an ax.

"Pete," he called, "Penny, come here."

Pete was having so much fun making tunnels in the dirt, he didn't want to answer.

Penny was having fun making houses in the dirt. She answered "What?" but she didn't jump up and run to Daddy as she knew she should when he called her.

"Pete," Daddy called again. "Penny."

Slowly the children came.

"Children, I want you to drag these branches over to the brush pile. After it rains and the woods aren't so dry, we can burn the branches."

"Aw," growled Pete. "I don't want to work. I'd rather play."

"Do we have to?" whined Penny. "You do it, Daddy."

Daddy put his ax down. He put one foot up on a log and reached for his New Testament. Two pouting children heard him read, " 'Children, obey your parents in all things: for this is well pleasing unto the Lord' (Colossians 3:20)."

13

"He loved me and sent His Son," thought Pete. *"I should do those things that are pleasing to God. I should obey Daddy."* Pete knew what he should do, but he still didn't want to do it. Out loud, he said. "OK Dad, I'll pile branches on the brush pile."

He picked up a long feathery branch in each hand and started to drag them away.

Penny sighed. Then she picked up a branch.

Pete and Penny were obeying Daddy. But they were not happy about it. They grumbled and growled and scowled.

"How much money are you going to give us," asked Pete, "for all this work we are doing?"

"No money at all," said Daddy. "Our whole family is going to live in the house, and our whole family will work to get it ready."

Daddy was busy chopping off branches, but he stopped long enough to read from his Bible, " 'For even when we were with you, this we commanded you, that if any would not work, neither should he eat' (2 Thessalonians 3:10)."

Pete and Penny both liked to eat.

"Pete," said Penny. "We'd better work. The Bible says if we won't work, we can't eat."

"Just one more thing," said Daddy. "Maybe you have forgotten that one fruit of the Spirit is joy. Do you remember Psalm 100? 'Serve the Lord with glad-

ness: come before his presence with singing' (Psalm 100:2). It is one thing to be glad on Sunday and sing in church. It is another thing to be glad while we work, and sing then."

Pete and Penny were ashamed of themselves.

They stopped scowling and growling. They piled brush and while they piled, they sang:

> Somebody 'round me, somebody near,
>   Needs the song I can sing:
> Somebody 'round me, somebody near,
>   Needs the love I can bring:
> Somebody 'round me, somebody near,
>   Needs to know Jesus, too;
> Somebody 'round me, somebody near,
>   Needs just what I can do.*

Lots of Fun Around the New House

AFTER THE BULLDOZER had dug a big hole in the ground, the carpenter came. He measured and tied long strings to stakes to be sure to get the house straight and square. Then he started to build forms. The forms were long narrow boxes made of boards.

*Primaries Sing, published by Scripture Press.

Cement would be poured into them and it would get hard. This was the beginning of a big basement.

While Daddy and the carpenter pounded, Pete and Penny played in big mountains of dirt that the bull-dozer had left. When Daddy had jobs they could do, Pete and Penny did them. When there were no jobs, they could play.

Pete brought his toy fire engine and truck and car, and he built roads and bridges and tunnels.

Penny made a house. She patted the damp dirt into walls. She made a table and a bed.

"I wish Janey were here," she said. "We used to have lots of fun together. It is more fun to do something with someone else, than just to be by yourself."

"I wish Bob would be friends," Pete added. "We would have fun digging tunnels."

Daddy stopped pounding nails and came over to see the things the children had made. He came in time to hear Pete say, "But I have tried twice to be friends. Janey is still the same stuckup, cross, mean old horrid person and Bob won't even look at me or talk. If that is the way they want to be, OK. I'm tired of being nice."

"Just a minute," said Daddy. "Let's see what God says about that. Don't forget that love, joy, peace, longsuffering, gentleness, goodness, and meekness are fruits of the Spirit."

Then Daddy turned to the New Testament he had in his pocket. " 'Love suffereth long, and is kind; love . . . seeketh not her own, is not easily provoked' (1 Corinthians 13:4-5)."

"What is *provoke?*" asked Penny.

"Well, Pete was just acting as if he were provoked," explained Daddy. "He said that he was tired of being nice, and he sounded pretty mad."

Pete ran his truck under a bridge, but he was listening.

"The three fruits of the Spirit called gentleness, goodness, and meekness are something alike," said Daddy. "They teach us that we should be kind."

"Well, God will have to help me a lot," said Pete. "I sure don't feel like being kind. Besides, I can't think of another way to be kind, and if I did think of something, I'd rather not do it. Who wants to be called names and hated?"

"Let's pray right now," Daddy suggested.

So Pete prayed: "Dear God, You know how hard it is to love Janey and Bob and be nice to them. Help me think of something kind to do and help me do it. In Jesus' name. Amen."

Penny smiled. While Pete was praying, she had prayed in her heart. She wanted the fruit of the Holy Spirit to be seen in her life, too.

The Foundation of the House Is Done

THE DAY the cement mixer came, Pete and Penny were excited. They stayed at the lot and watched the truck roll in with its big barrel going around and around.

The driver put the chute down to the forms, pushed a button, and out came the cement. The gooey gray mixture of stones and sand and cement flowed down. And two men pushed it into the right places with long shovels.

Time after time, the cement mixer came bringing more cement.

That night at the table, Pete and Penny told Mother how much fun they had. "It would have been more fun," said Pete, "if Bob and Janey had been there. I wish we were friends like we used to be."

"You prayed," said Penny, "that God would help you think of something kind to do." Then Penny turned to Daddy, "Does it really do any good to pray? Does God hear? Are things different after we pray?"

"One question at a time." Daddy reached for his Bible. "Does God hear when we pray? This verse tells us, 'The eyes of the Lord are upon the righteous, and his ears are open unto their cry' (Psalm 34:15)."

"Who are the righteous?" asked Penny.

"The righteous are the people who belong to God because they have been born into His family and want to follow His right ways," replied Daddy. "God sees them and He hears them when they call on Him."

"Why do we always say 'In Jesus' Name' at the end of a prayer?" asked Penny.

"God the Father is the one to whom we pray," answered Daddy. "But He sent Jesus to die for our sins so that we could belong to God's family by believing on Jesus and thus be God's friends. God accepts us because of what Jesus did for us. That is why we pray in Jesus' Name."

"I am going to pray every day for Janey," declared Penny, "until she is saved and we are friends. It makes me sad when she is mad. I'll pray that she will want to go to Sunday school with me. I'll pray that her folks will let her."

And Penny prayed with all her heart.

Watching the House Grow

AFTER THE CEMENT was hard, Daddy helped the carpenter to rip off the boards. These boards could be used for the floor of the kitchen and the front room and the bedrooms. A little cement still stuck to them. Scraping it off was a good job for Pete and Penny. With the sharp prongs of the hammers, they scraped and cleaned the boards.

It was fun to watch the house grow. It was fun to help.

"Next week school starts," sighed Pete. "I like school, but I'll miss being at the lot."

"You can come over after school, and maybe after supper," said Daddy. "We want to work as fast as we can, so we can move into our new house before the cold weather comes."

"Before Thanksgiving?" asked Penny.

"Before Thanksgiving, the Lord willing," said Daddy.

"Why do you say 'the Lord willing'?" asked Penny.

"Because," said Daddy, "lots of things could happen before then to delay the building. I don't even know what will happen tomorrow. Listen to this verse."

> Go to now, ye that say, Today or tomorrow we will go into such a city, and continue there a year, and buy and sell, and get gain: whereas ye know not what shall be on the morrow . . . For that ye ought to say, If the Lord will, we shall live, and do this, or that (James 4:13-15).

21

"Well," said Penny, "I surely hope God *is* willing. I can't wait to move into our new house."

The boards that had held the cement had been nailed with double-headed nails. A little bit of nail with an extra head stuck out of each board. They were easy to pull out.

"Want to try?" asked Daddy. The boards on one side of the basement still had to be taken off.

"Sure," said Pete.

"Sure," said Penny.

They tugged and pulled, and one by one the nails came out.

"Daddy," began Penny, "does God answer every single prayer of a saved person?"

"He answers every one," said Daddy. "Only He doesn't always say yes. If you'd ask me if you may play with a sharp knife, I would say no."

"Once," said Pete, "I asked for a football. You answered, 'I will give you something better.' Then you gave me a bicycle."

"Sometimes I ask for a cooky," said Penny, "and Mother says, 'Wait a while. After supper you may have one.' "

"That is very much the way God answers prayer," explained Daddy. "Sometimes His answer is yes, sometimes, no, sometimes, 'something better,' and sometimes, 'wait a while!' "

"God knows best," said Penny. "But sometimes it is hard to understand His answers. It is hard to wait. I wonder when Janey will be friends again? I wonder when she will go to Sunday school with me?"

Penny Tries to Be Friendly

PETE AND PENNY were excited the day school started. It was fun to wear their new school clothes. Penny had a plaid blouse just like Pete's red plaid shirt. She wore a pleated blue skirt, the same blue as his pants. It was fun to see the new teacher and their old friends. There were a few new kids to get acquainted with, too.

Pete sat behind Penny, and Janey sat two rows away. When Janey looked at her, Penny smiled. But Janey did not smile. She put her nose up in the air and looked at Penny the way she would have looked at a horrid, wriggling snake. Then she turned her head away.

"Dear God," whispered Penny, "help her not to hate me. Help me to love her and be kind. In Jesus' Name. Amen."

At recess, Penny ran up behind Janey and slipped her hand into Janey's and squeezed it.

"It's fun to pull nails out of the boards at our new house," she said. "Can you come over after school? Please do."

Janey only snatched her hand away as if she had been touching nettles that sting, and ran away.

Penny felt like crying. In fact, a big tear came, spilled over, and ran down her pink cheek.

Quickly Penny brushed the tear away with the back of her hand, but the ache was still there.

That night after supper, Pete and Penny and Daddy and Mother sat in the front room by the fireplace. Daddy popped corn. Penny stirred in the melted butter. Pete sprinkled on the salt.

"Daddy," asked Penny, "what prayers does God say yes to? Will He help Janey and me ever to be friends?"

Daddy reached for His Bible. He read, "Ye have not, because ye ask not. Ye ask, and receive not, because ye ask amiss, that ye may consume it upon your lusts" (James 4:2-3).

"Sometimes," explained Daddy, "we want things, and don't have them, because we don't pray and ask God for them. Or maybe we'll pray only once or twice. Sometimes we ask and don't get what we ask for, because we are selfish and really want the things we pray for, only for our own enjoyment."

Then Daddy turned to another place in his Bible and read:

> And this is the confidence that we have in him, that, if we ask anything according to his will, he heareth us: and if we know that he hear us, whatsoever we ask, we know that we have the petitions that we desired of him (1 John 5:14-15).

"Is it God's will that Janey and I be friends?" asked Penny.

"I am sure it is," replied Mother. "He wants us to love one another. It is His will that Janey love you and that you love Janey."

"It must be God's will for Bob and me to be friends, too," said Pete. "I wonder when we will be?"

"Don't stop praying," said Mother. "God will hear and answer."

"I hope it will be soon," Penny sighed. "I'll be glad when we are friends again."

A New Puppy for Janey and Bob

PETE AND PENNY were waiting for Daddy to come out to the car. They had eaten supper early so they could work on the new house for a couple of hours before it got dark.

"Look," said Pete. "Mr. Barber is just getting home from work."

They heard Mr. Barber call Janey and Bob, then saw them dash out of the house. They saw Mr. Barber take a big box from the car, and then they heard a "Yip, yip, yip."

Pete and Penny watched Janey and Bob peek into the box.

"He's cute," they heard Janey say. "Daddy, he is a darling puppy."

"Boy, oh boy," exclaimed Bob. "A cocker spaniel. Just the kind of dog I wanted."

As Pete and Penny and Daddy drove away, they saw Janey and Bob carry the box with their new pet into the house.

"I wonder what color it is?" said Pete.

"Honey brown," said Penny. "I saw his head and his paws. They were the color of golden honey."

"Now they won't care if they never make up to us." Pete pouted. "They will just play with their old puppy."

"I haven't forgotten how nasty Janey was to me in school yesterday," said Penny. "I pretended not to care, but I did care. Who wants to be treated like poison?"

"Let's not try to be friends," said Pete. "If they

28

want to hate us, let's hate them. I get tired of praying for them. It doesn't do any good."

"I'm tired of being kind, too," agreed Penny. "The hateful old redhead!"

Daddy was driving the car. He said nothing, but he was listening. When they came to the new house, the children were going to jump out and start to pull nails, but Daddy said, "Wait a minute."

He took out his Bible and read, " 'If I regard iniquity in my heart, the Lord will not hear me' (Psalm 66:18)."

Then Daddy explained, *"Iniquity* is another word for sin, you remember. If you have sin in your hearts, the Lord will not hear you when you pray."

"We haven't been bad," protested Penny.

"You just said you were tired of being kind, and you talked about hating your neighbors," replied Daddy. Then he read, " 'Be ye kind one to another, tenderhearted, forgiving one another, even as God for Christ's sake hath forgiven you' (Ephesians 4:32)."

"If God has forgiven you because of what Christ did, you surely can forgive Janey and Bob and keep on being kind."

Right in the car, Penny prayed, "Dear God, I am sorry. Help me not to say or even think mean things. Help me to forgive Janey for being so horrid to me. Help me to be kind. In Jesus' Name. Amen."

The New Puppy Is Lost

IT WAS DARK when Pete and Penny and Daddy drove into the garage, and it had started to rain.

On their way to the porch, they heard Janey ask, "Which way do you think he went? Oh, my poor puppy. Where are you?"

Bob's voice answered. "How do I know which way he went? Why did you open the door, stupid?"

Penny gasped. "Their new puppy is lost already!"

"Bob. Hey Bob," called Pete. "Shall I get a flashlight and help you find your dog?"

"You don't need to bother," yelled Janey. "We'll hunt for our own dog."

Inside the house, Pete and Penny talked it over with Mother and Daddy.

"You prayed for a way to be kind to Bob and Janey," said Mother. "This is a good chance."

"But that snippy old Janey yelled at us and told us not to bother," protested Pete.

"But that poor little puppy," said Penny, "is out there in the dark and the cold."

"And the rain," added Mother. "It is really raining now."

"If we found their puppy, they might be friends," said Penny.

30

"I'll go with you," said Daddy, "if you want to look."

"But we don't know which way to start out," said Pete.

"Can we pray about that?" asked Penny. "Daddy, is it all right to pray about a little lost puppy?"

Daddy answered that question by reaching for his Bible. He read:

> In nothing be anxious, but in everything by prayer and supplication with thanksgiving let your requests be made known unto God. And the peace of God, which passeth all understanding, shall guard your hearts and your thoughts in Christ Jesus (Philippians 4:6-7, R.V.).

"It means," explained Daddy, "that Christians should not worry about anything. God is interested in everything we do. There is not one thing in our lives that we cannot talk to God about."

"And we must remember to thank Him for help," said Penny.

Mother added, "We know that God will answer and do what is the very best."

So Pete and Penny prayed.

"Dear God," began Pete, "You know just where that little lost puppy is this very second. It's dark and wet outside, and we don't know where he is, but You do. Please help us find him. In Jesus' Name. Amen."

"Dear God," prayed Penny, "it is cold and wet outside, and it would be cozy to get into our warm beds. But please help us find the puppy first. In Jesus' Name. Amen."

Then Pete and Penny had peace in their hearts. They knew that God had heard. They knew that He would help them.

Pete and Penny Look for the Puppy

PETE AND PENNY and Daddy stood on the porch wondering which way to go. Each one had on boots and a raincoat, and each had a flashlight.

"Janey and Bob and their Dad went toward the park," said Pete. "We better start out toward the school."

"We can't call him," said Penny. "We don't know his name."

"He probably doesn't know his name either" said Pete. "He is so new."

"Puppy," called Penny. "Here puppy, here puppy. Where are you?" She flashed her light behind a bush.

33

Slish, slosh, slish, slosh, went their boots on the wet pavement and in the puddles.

They passed a big man with his hands in his pockets and his coat collar turned up around his ears.

"Pardon me," said Pete, "but have you seen a little lost puppy?"

"Not one," said the man, and on he went.

On porches, under bushes, behind walls, beside houses, they flashed their lights. No honey-colored puppy.

"He has to be somewhere," said Pete.

"God knows where he is," said Penny, "and we asked Him to help us find him."

"Maybe Bob and Janey found him already," said Pete.

"Let's look a little more," said Penny, "but not for long. I'm cold and wet. I'm so tired and hungry."

Pete flashed his light on a lawn, "What if we do find him? Will Bob and Janey be glad or mad?"

"Let's find him first."

"He couldn't have come this far. Let's go around the block and head for home," Pete said.

On and on Pete and Penny and Daddy trudged in the wet and the cold.

"It's no use," sighed Penny. "Let's just hurry home. Let's not look any more."

34

But Pete wouldn't give up. He whistled. "Here pup!" he called.

Then he heard a little whine.

"Pup! Where are you?" Pete flashed his light around. The light fell on a big, big pipe that the sewer men were going to use. Pete heard another little whine. He leaned over and looked inside the pipe. There was the honey-colored puppy!

"Here puppy, here puppy," Pete called, but the puppy would not budge.

"He's afraid," said Pete. "Hold the light, Penny. I'll have to crawl in after him."

Pete wiggled and wormed himself inside the big pipe. At last he grabbed the little puppy and backed out.

Shivering and shaking, the dog yipped and whined and licked Pete's face. Pete tucked him under his raincoat and held him close.

"God answered our prayer," said Penny.

Daddy said, " 'O give thanks unto the LORD; for he is good . . . I love the LORD, because he hath heard my voice . . . Because he hath inclined his ear unto me, therefore will I call upon him as long as I live' (Psalm 118:1; 116:1-2)."

"I am glad we prayed about finding the puppy," said Pete. "I am glad God helped us find him."

A Happy Time Next Door

DADDY WENT HOME. It would be best to let Pete and Penny meet Janey and Bob by themselves.

Pete and Penny stood on the front porch of the Barber house. The wet, lost little puppy that was found was tucked inside Pete's coat. Pete pushed the button that rang the doorbell.

While Pete and Penny waited they wondered. Would Bob and Janey be friends with them now? Or would they be glad to see the puppy but stay mad at them?

Penny could hear footsteps inside the house. Then the door opened. There stood Janey in her robe, ready for bed. Her eyes were red from crying.

Bob bounced down the stairs behind her. He looked mad and sad.

Janey opened her mouth in surprise. She had not expected to find Pete and Penny standing on the front porch. Not after she had been so mean to them and had thrown rocks at them and had told them to stay on their side of the fence. What could they want?

Then Pete pulled open his coat.

"Honey! You found our Honey!" Janey squealed.

Bob beamed. How glad he was to see that puppy again!

Mr. Barber came to the door. "Ask the children in," he said.

Inside, Janey took Honey from Pete and stroked the soft hair behind the puppy's ears. She rubbed her cheek on the top of his head and held him close.

"I thought you were lost for good," she said.

"Where did you find him?" asked Bob. "We hunted and hunted, but we had to give up."

"In a big pipe. We found your puppy in a pipe," Penny said.

Just then, Mrs. Barber came in with cookies and cocoa.

"You children are cold and you must be hungry. Take your coats off and eat."

Janey sat on the rug and hugged her dog, but she was quiet. She was thinking. Then she said, "Why did you look for our puppy? Why did you walk around in the cold and the dark and the wet? We have been so mean and so hateful and so horrid. Why—?"

Pete swallowed a bite of cooky.

"Because," he said, "we love God. We belong to Him. We are His children because we both took the Lord Jesus Christ as our own Saviour this summer."

"We prayed," Penny said simply. "We asked God

to help us do something to show you that we love you and that God loves you. We wish you would go to Sunday school with us."

"I'm sorry," Janey said. "I'm sorry I threw rocks. I'm not happy when I throw rocks and yell mean things. I want to be nice, like you." She looked at her mother and then at her father. "I wish I could go to Sunday school."

Janey's folks nodded their heads.

"The twins have something we need at our house," Mr. Barber said. "We have left God out of our lives. We won't do it any more."

It was late. Pete and Penny thanked the Barbers for the cookies and cocoa. The Barbers thanked Pete and Penny for finding their puppy. Then the children ran home.

They told Daddy and Mother the good news.

"They aren't mad any more, and they want to go to Sunday school," blurted Pete joyfully.

As usual Daddy was ready with just the right Bible verse. He read:

> Thus saith the LORD . . . Call unto me, and I will answer thee, and show thee great and mighty things, which thou knowest not (Jeremiah 33:2-3).

Then Pete and Penny thanked God for hearing and answering their prayers.

Payday for Pete and Penny

On Saturday, Pete and Penny worked hard all morning over at the new house. The carpenter had sawed the boards just the right size for the first floor. Daddy nailed them down. Pete and Penny handed the nails to Daddy.

With the children helping, the work went faster. They did not grumble or growl or scowl. They sang while they worked. They sang their favorite song:

> Somebody 'round me, somebody near,
>> Needs the song I can sing:
> Somebody 'round me, somebody near,
>> Needs the love I can bring:
> Somebody 'round me, somebody near,
>> Needs to know Jesus, too;
> Somebody 'round me, somebody near,
>> Needs just what I can do.

At noon Daddy stopped pounding. He stood up. "Pete and Penny," he said, "you have worked hard all morning. You have been cheerful about it. Today I will pay you for working."

That was a happy surprise. The children knew that the house was for the whole family to live in. They knew that they would not be paid for every

40

41

job they did. But it was nice to have money of their own.

Daddy reached into his pocket. He gave each of the children a quarter.

"Boy," Pete said. "Thanks, Dad. A whole quarter all for myself. A whole quarter to spend on anything I want."

"Remember that part of that quarter belongs to God," reminded Daddy.

"How come?" asked Pete. "I earned it, didn't I? How come I can't spend it all on myself if I want to?"

"If you want to, you can," Daddy replied. "Nobody will make you or Penny give part of your quarters back to God, but it would make God happy if you give Him part of it because you want to."

Daddy took out his Bible and read, " 'Every man according as he purposeth in his heart, so let him give; not grudgingly, or of necessity: for God loveth a cheerful giver' (2 Corinthians 9:7)."

"How can we give money to God?" asked Penny. "He doesn't need money to buy things."

"But His children do," said Daddy. "Missionaries are people who spend most of their time telling people who have not heard about Jesus how they can be saved. They need money to buy food. You cannot give money to God Himself, but if you give money to missionaries who love Him, God counts it the same as giving it to Him."

"How much of my quarter shall I give?" asked Pete.

"It isn't 'how much' shall we give," said Daddy. "When we belong to the Lord all that we have is already His. In the Old Testament days God's people were required to give one tenth of their income and that was called a tithe." Daddy opened his Bible and read:

> Bring ye all the tithes into the storehouse, that there may be meat in mine house, and prove me now herewith, saith the Lord of hosts, if I will not open the windows of heaven, and pour you out a blessing, that there shall not be room enough to receive it (Malachi 3:10).

"Here the people were promised blessing as they gave to the Lord."

"What is a tenth of twenty-five cents?" asked Penny.

"It's two and a half cents," chimed in Pete. "I figured that out."

"I'll give God five cents, for good measure," said Penny and Daddy smiled. She was glad she could give five cents to God. Didn't she have twenty cents left for herself?

Janey Makes a Decision

SATURDAY AFTERNOON, Pete and Penny played at the lot. This time Janey and Bob played with them.

Pete and Bob made tunnels and bridges and winding roads in the damp dirt for their trucks and trailers.

"I'm glad you came," Pete said. "This is more fun than playing alone."

Penny and Janey made a real tunnel in the big pile of evergreen branches. They pulled branches and pushed them, until there was a place where they could crawl in.

"This is cozy," Janey said. "It smells good, too. I like the smell of evergreen branches."

"I know how to make it cozier," Penny said. "There is an old blanket by the picnic table. It will be all right if we use it."

The girls spread the blanket inside their little evergreen house. It was like a soft nest. They snuggled down in it together.

"I am glad," said Penny, "that we are friends again."

Janey did not answer for a minute. Then she said, "I am glad you forgave me when I said I was sorry for being so horrid. But I still don't feel happy deep down in my heart."

"You need to take the Lord Jesus Christ as your very own Saviour," Penny answered. "Then you can be happy."

"I'm glad I can go to Sunday school tomorrow," Janey said. "Maybe if I go to Sunday school I will learn about Jesus."

"Lots of children believe in Jesus at Sunday school," Penny told Janey. "But you don't need to wait until tomorrow. You can become a Christian right now if you want to be."

"Can I really?"

"Sure, I'll ask Daddy."

Mr. Pendleton was busy pounding nails. But he was not too busy to stop and tell a little girl how to know the Lord.

He sat on a pile of lumber. Janey sat on one side of him and Penny on the other. He opened his Bible and pointed to a verse. Out loud, Janey read:

> All we like sheep have gone astray; we have turned every one to his own way; and the LORD hath laid on him the iniquity of us all (Isaiah 53:6).

"Like lost sheep," said Daddy, "all of us have gone our own way, which is far from God. But God loved us and sent His Son. On Him was laid the iniquity— that means the sin—of us all."

"Did Jesus take the punishment for my sins?" asked Janey.

"He did," answered Daddy.

"Right now, I believe that Jesus died to save me," Janey said.

Then she bowed her head and shut her eyes. "Dear God," Janey began, "thank you that Jesus died for *me.* Amen."

Penny got up and gave Janey a hug.

Daddy opened to another verse:

> That if thou shalt confess with thy mouth the Lord Jesus, and shalt believe in thine heart that God hath raised him from the dead, thou shalt be saved. For with the heart man believeth unto righteousness; and with the mouth confession is made unto salvation (Romans 10:9-10).

"I've already believed in my heart. With my mouth I will tell Pete and Bob," Janey said. "I'm glad that I'm saved, that I know the Lord Jesus, like you do. I will be glad to tell everybody."

Bob Stops a Bad Habit

PETE AND PENNY were happy when they heard Janey tell her brother Bob that she was a Christian.

47

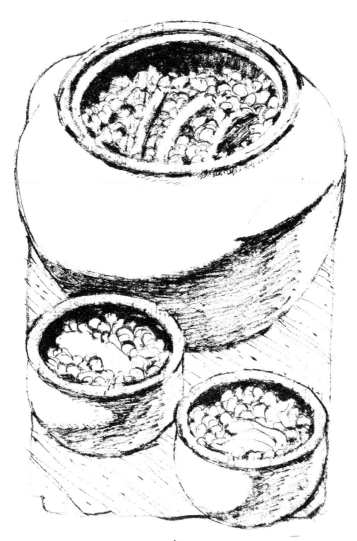

48

Bob wanted to be saved from eternal punishment too. So Mr. Pendleton showed him some Bible verses which explained to Bob that he was a sinner who needed to be saved. "'For the Son of man is come to seek and to save that which was lost' (Luke 19:10)."

Soon Bob believed that the Lord Jesus Christ, God's only Son, had died for him.

Daddy went back to pounding nails.

The boys went back to play in the dirt.

The girls went back to play in the pile of evergreen brush.

They were all happy and glad.

After a while, they saw a car drive in. Mother had come with a picnic supper.

The girls helped her unpack the food and set the picnic table.

"Come," called Penny. "Come to supper."

Daddy and the boys came.

"Gee, it smells good," Bob said. "Golly. How did you know I like baked beans?"

Soon they were all seated. Daddy asked Pete to thank God for the food. Then they ate. There were beans and sliced tomatoes, and wedges of cheese, and cantaloupe and green grapes.

"We are saved, Mrs. Pendleton," blurted out

49

Janey. "Bob and I both took Jesus as our Saviour this afternoon."

Mother smiled. "I'm glad. We have prayed for you for a long time."

"Now that you are saved," said Daddy, "you will want to please God by everything you say and do."

"That's right," agreed Bob.

"One of the ten commandments, which are rules to help us live so we can please God," continued Daddy, "says this: 'Thou shalt not take the name of the Lord thy God in vain' (Exodus 20:7)."

"That means," explained Daddy, "that we can use the name of God or Jesus when we want to pray or speak about them in a nice way, but never, never should we say the name of Jesus to swear when we hit our thumbs with the hammer or get mad or just for fun."

"Why are you telling us this?" asked Penny. "Who has been swearing?"

"I heard someone say 'gee' and 'golly,'" replied Daddy. "*Gee* is a nickname for Jesus. *Golly* and *gosh* are naughty ways to say *God. The dickens* is a way to speak of the devil. *Darn* means *to curse,* to wish harm to someone. When we know God and love Him, we don't use those words anymore."

"I have used those words so long," said Bob, "it

50

is a habit. It is a bad habit. I will ask God to help me not to say them anymore, ever."

Four Children Go to Sunday School

PETE AND PENNY stood on the Barbers' front porch. They wore their best brown brother-and-sister suits that matched their brown eyes. Pete pushed the button that rang the doorbell. The last time they had stood there, they had been afraid, wondering. Now they were happy and glad. They were ready to go to Sunday school and Janey and Bob were to go with them.

The door opened and Jane smiled. Bob bounced down the stairs behind her, and soon all four children were in the Pendleton car on their way to Sunday school.

"I'm glad you were both ready," Pete said. "I like to be at Sunday school on time. It is even good to be a little early."

"I am never late to school," replied Bob. "Our mother gets us up in time so we won't be."

"If we poke, she reminds us to hurry," said Janey.

"She tells us she was never late to school in her life and she doesn't want us to be."

"School is important," Penny agreed. "Sunday school is even more important. That is why we do our best to be on time."

When they arrived, many boys and girls and men and women were climbing the stairs that led inside the little white church.

Soft music was playing in the room where the children went. Already sitting there were other children their same age. Just as the hand on the big clock on the wall pointed to a quarter to ten, the superintendent stood up and smiled. She read a verse from her big Bible: " 'I was glad when they said unto me, Let us go into the house of the LORD' (Psalm 122:1)."

I am glad, too, thought Janey. *I have often wondered what folks do in church. Today I'll find out.*

Then she listened while the others sang. The words of the song were Bible words, from Habakkuk 2:20: " 'The LORD is in his holy temple: let all the earth keep silence before him.' "*

The children sang the same song a second time, with their heads bowed and their eyes closed. Then a teacher prayed, "Dear God, we are glad we could come to Your house on Your day. Help us to love

Primaries Sing, published by Scripture Press.

52

53

You better because we have come here. In Jesus' Name. Amen."

Jane and Bob could not sing, because they did not know the words, but they listened. Janey liked the words of the song called "My Best Friend."*

> Anytime, anywhere, I can talk to God,
> When I'm glad, when I'm sad, I can talk
>   to God.
> Sometimes on my knees I pray,
> Sometimes as I work or play,
> When I need Him through the day,
> My best Friend is He.

"You don't have to be in church to pray," said the smiling lady in front. "You don't have to wait until you kneel by your bed at night. Anytime, anywhere, you can talk to God. You can talk to Him when you are glad or when you are sad. He is your very best Friend."

Janey's heart was full of happiness. It was true. God was her best Friend. Hadn't He sent His only Son, the Lord Jesus Christ, to die for her and to take the punishment she deserved?

The lady in front was reading another verse from her Bible: " 'O give thanks unto the LORD, for he is good' (Psalm 107:1)."

*Primaries Sing, published by Scripture Press.

I will give thanks, thought Janey. *I will give thanks unto the Lord.* She smiled at Penny and squeezed her hand.

Pete Finds a Pocketknife

PETE AND PENNY waited at the gate for Bob and Janey. It was Monday morning. Janey flew out the door, and Bob bounced down the stairs behind her.

"I brought my new knife along," puffed Bob. "I want to show it to you."

Pete's eyes popped. "Boy, it's a beauty! Let me see it."

Pete fingered the shiny white knife. It had a picture of a cowboy painted in red on the handle. He opened the three blades.

"Good and sharp," he said. "It even has a can opener. Boy, I would love to have a knife like that!"

He shut the blades and watched Bob slip it into his pocket.

Pete walked along. He did not say much all the rest of the way to school. *Some guys get everything,* he thought. *A three-bladed knife with a red cowboy on the handle. Boy!*

The children were ten minutes early. They had

time to play on the bars. Pete climbed, with the others, like a monkey, but his thoughts were on that shiny knife.

"Look!" shouted Bob. "This is a new trick. I can hang by my knees."

Then the bell rang. Everyone dashed to get in line.

Pete had been at the top of the bars, so he was the last one down. Just as he started to run toward the building, he saw something on the ground. It was shiny white with a splotch of red. It couldn't be—but it was. When Bob had hung by his knees, it must have slipped out of his pocket.

Pete snatched up the knife and stuck it into his own pocket. He glanced around. He was the last one on the playground. No one had seen him find it.

Finders keepers, losers weepers, he thought. *I've always wanted a knife like this. Bob won't know where he lost it, and he won't know who found it. I'll keep quiet. I won't say a word, and he will never know.*

That night, after supper, Pete patted his pocket. Yes, it was still there. He took the knife out to look at it.

Daddy looked over his shoulder. "Where did you get the knife, son?"

Startled, Pete jumped. He had not heard Daddy come in.

"Oh," answered Pete. "I found it. I just found it."

Penny came in. "Found what? That knife? That is Bob's knife. You stole it from him."

"I did not. I found it."

"Do you know who it belongs to?" asked Daddy.

Pete looked down. "Yes," he said in a low voice.

"If you know who it belongs to, don't you think you had better give it back?"

"I found it," Pete mumbled. "I didn't steal it. I found it on the playground and I want to keep it."

Daddy opened his Bible and read, " 'And as ye would that men should do to you, do ye also to them likewise' (Luke 6:31)."

Pete was silent for three whole minutes. Finally, he said, "I will take the knife back to Bob. If I lost a knife and Bob found it, I would want him to give it back to me."

So Pete did.

58

An Invitation to the Farm

PETE AND PENNY had an invitation. Bob and Janey had asked them to go to their uncle's farm on Saturday.

"He has a pet lion," Bob told them. "It was born in the zoo. When it was still tiny, it got sick and the zoo-keeper thought it would die. He told my Uncle Alfred he could take it home."

"He fed it with a medicine dropper at first," Janey said. "It got stronger, and then he fed it with a baby bottle."

"It is a big lion now, but it is tame as a dog," Bob added. "It walks all around the house and yard."

"I hope we can go," Penny sighed. "I sure hope Daddy and Mother will let us go." She ran to ask.

"If your grades are good at school all week," promised Daddy, "you may go to see the tame lion. I am sure Mother will agree to that."

"My grades are most always pretty good," Penny said.

"You can do good work if you want to," said Daddy, "but sometimes you are careless. Sometimes you don't think. Do your best all week."

Penny decided she just had to get good grades. She had to see that tame lion.

In school the teacher told the class, "Study your spelling words for fifteen minutes. Then we shall have a spelling test."

I want to get 100, thought Penny. *I want to see the lion.*

But instead of studying, Penny looked out of the window and thought about the lion. Not once did she look at the spelling words or practice writing them.

"Clear your desks," the teacher said. "Get your papers and pencils ready."

"Farmer," said the teacher.

"F-a-r-m-e-r," spelled Penny.

She could spell *house* and *bear*, too. They were easy words.

"Indian," said the teacher.

Oh, gulped Penny. *That is a hard one.* She chewed the end of her pencil. She looked out of the window. She still could not spell it. Then she had an idea. Teacher was writing on the blackboard. Penny sneaked a quick look at Pete's paper.

"I-n-d-i-a-n," she spelled.

When the papers were corrected, she looked at her grade.

"Good," she said. "I got 100. I want to see the lion."

On Friday, Daddy looked at the children's work

for the week. "Your grades are good," he said. "You may both go to see the lion."

But Penny felt sick inside. She had not deserved 100 in spelling. She had cheated. Finally, she told Daddy.

"Cheating is acting a lie," said Daddy. "It is stealing off another's paper, too."

Then Daddy read from his Bible:

> If we confess our sins, he is faithful and just to forgive us our sins, and to cleanse us from all unrighteousness (1 John 1:9).

Penny kneeled by a chair. "Dear God," she began, "I am sorry I cheated. Please wash my sin away. In Jesus' Name. Amen."

No One Can Hide from God

AFTER PENNY had asked God to forgive her for cheating in the spelling test, she felt a little better. Hadn't God promised that if she would confess her sin to Him, He would forgive her and wash the sin away?

But the matter was not settled. Penny had one more thing to do. Miss Holly, her teacher, still had

"100" marked in her grade book for Penny's spelling. She would have to tell her that she had cheated.

"But I don't want to tell her," Penny argued. "I go to school dressed so pretty, with my hair brushed shiny and a bright bow tucked in it. I look nice on the outside. I answer most of the questions right so she says I am a good pupil. I don't want Miss Holly to know what a horrid girl I am inside. I don't want to tell her I cheated in spelling."

"Don't be too proud to admit you were wrong," Mother told her. "It is pride in your heart that makes you feel like keeping still when you know you should tell your teacher. In the Bible in the book of Proverbs, God tells us that there are six things that He hates. A proud look and a lying tongue are two of them. Listen: " 'An high look, and a proud heart . . . is sin' (Proverbs 21:4)."

Penny sat on the kitchen stool and thought. She knew God had forgiven her. Mother had read a verse that said, "As far as the east is from the west, so far hath he removed our transgression from us" (Psalm 103:12).

Penny knew that *transgression* was another word for sin. She knew the east was 'way over where the sun comes up. She knew that the west was 'way over where the sun goes down. She knew God had taken her sins that far away. Yet she still had to go to Miss Holly.

"Help me do what is right," she prayed.

Then she ran back to school. Perhaps Miss Holly would still be there correcting papers.

"Miss Holly," panted Penny, as she burst into the room.

Surprised, Miss Holly looked up from her desk.

"I . . ." Penny began. She lowered her eyes. She bit her lip and twisted her hanky. "I cheated," she blurted. "I did not deserve '100' in spelling. I looked on Pete's paper. I did not really know how to spell 'Indian.'"

"Thank you for telling me," Miss Holly said. "If you had not told me, I never would have known." She erased the grade from her book and wrote down "95."

"But God knew," replied Penny. "No one can hide from God." Then she added, "I don't want anything that doesn't belong to me. I don't want to steal a nickel or a pretty hanky or an eraser, and I don't want to steal work off Pete's paper to get a good grade that isn't really mine."

Then Penny smiled. God had forgiven her and Miss Holly had put the right grade in her book.

On the way home she skipped, and as she skipped she prayed, "Help me to do right, dear God."

Off to See the Lion

PETE AND PENNY woke up early on Saturday morning.

"The lion! Today we get to see the tame lion," said Penny.

Pete protested. "Does Penny get to go, Daddy? You said we had to have good grades to go and Penny cheated."

"I said good grades, not perfect grades," answered Daddy, "and 95 is a good grade. Penny missed only one word in spelling. Besides, I am glad that she was brave enough to tell me that she had cheated. I'm glad that she asked God to forgive her and that she told Miss Holly what she had done. We won't mention it anymore."

Daddy opened his Bible and read: " 'I, even I, am he that blotteth out thy transgressions for mine own sake, and will not remember thy sins' (Isaiah 43: 25)."

Then Daddy added, "If God promises to blot out our sins and not remember them anymore, surely we shouldn't remember them either."

Penny was glad. Cheating had brought her nothing but trouble and unhappiness. She would forget about it and not do it again.

65

Bob and Janey and Pete and Penny were soon in Mr. Barber's car on their way to see the lion. Out into the country they drove. The car turned in at a farm, then stopped. Bob bounced out with the others right behind.

Uncle Alfred was glad to see them.

"The lion," blurted Bob. "Where is the lion, Uncle Alfred?"

Just then an animal the size of a big, big dog came bounding around from behind the barn.

Penny squealed.

Janey squealed, too.

Uncle Alfred laughed. "Lena won't hurt you. Playful as a kitten."

He rubbed the lion under her chin and then scratched behind her ears.

"Come on, Lena. Let's show them the farm."

With Lena the lion at his heels, Uncle Alfred led the children to the edge of the woods. Many leaves had turned yellow. Some were bright red. It was fun to scuff their feet in the crunchy brown leaves on the ground.

Suddenly a terrible screech made them all jump.

Uncle Alfred laughed. "Peacocks are pretty, but they can't sing."

"Did that screech come from a peacock?" asked Penny.

Then she saw the big bird, his blue and green feathers spread in a huge fan. Around and around he strutted.

Penny picked up a feather that fell from the fan.

"I will keep it to remember the day I saw a tame lion and a live peacock," she said.

That night, Daddy listened while the children told about their trip.

Then he said, "Listen to what the Bible says about lions:

> The young lions do lack, and suffer hunger: but they that seek the LORD shall not want any good thing (Psalm 34:10).

A Silver Dollar for Penny

PETE AND PENNY sat down at the breakfast table.

Today Penny's brown curls were caught back with a jeweled clip.

"Oh, boy! Cantaloupe!" said Pete. "I want the biggest piece."

After Daddy thanked the Lord for the food, Pete reached over and helped himself to the biggest piece of the cantaloupe before he passed the platter to Penny.

"Your lunches are packed," Mother told them, "all

except the apples. Run to the basement, Pete, as soon as you are through breakfast, and get an apple to put in each lunch box."

When he had eaten his breakfast, Pete did as he was told.

"Two juicy apples," he panted. "I'll put the biggest and reddest in my pail," he added under his breath.

After school, the children ran home. Pete was the first to discover two glasses of milk and two pieces of cake waiting for them on the kitchen table.

"Good for Mom," said Pete. "She knows we're always hungry. I'll just grab this bigger piece before Penny does."

The children sat on kitchen stools and ate their snacks.

Pete gobbled his big piece of cake and gulped his milk.

Penny nibbled her little piece of cake. She bit something hard.

"What's this?" she asked. "What's in my cake? Why, it's something wrapped in wax paper." She looked. "It's money!" she gasped. "A silver dollar. A whole dollar!"

"A silver dollar?" echoed Pete. "How did money get in your piece of cake?"

Mother was darning socks in the next room.

"I put it there," she said.

"How come?" demanded Pete. "How come Penny got a silver dollar in her cake, and I didn't?"

"You could have had that piece of cake if you had wanted it," Mother replied. "You were the first one in the kitchen, and you took the piece you wanted. Penny had no choice. She took the piece you left."

That night Daddy was told about the money in the cake. Penny was pleased, but Pete was still pouting.

"It was a plot Mother and I planned," confessed Daddy. "We have noticed a boy around here who always says, 'I want the biggest. I want the best. I want to be first.'" Then Daddy opened his Bible and read, "'Be kindly affectioned one to another with brotherly love; in honor preferring one another' (Romans 12:10)."

"To prefer," explained Daddy, "means that you consider the other person's interests more than you do your own, and you want him or her to have the best. That is real brotherly love. To say with your lips that you love your sister is one thing. To show it by your actions is another."

"I made fudge," said Mother. "Pete, you may pass it."

There was one piece bigger than the others. In-

69

stead of snatching it before he passed the plate, Pete offered it to Penny.

"You take the biggest piece this time," he said.

Pete Becomes a Businessman

PETE WAS PRETTY PROUD of himself. He had a job—a paper route. It was a real job, and at the end of every month he would have ten dollars. Ten dollars! That was a lot of money for a boy Pete's age.

"The manager is not going to give you the money for nothing," warned Daddy. "You will have to earn it."

"It will be easy," Pete boasted.

The first morning he jumped up when the alarm went off and pulled on his clothes. He had a job and he would do it right.

The second morning he stayed in bed only a minute after the alarm bell woke him, before he got up. But the third morning Pete was so sleepy that when the alarm bell rang, he pushed the button that turned it off and went to sleep again.

Later, Mother came in. "Pete! Are you still here? Jump up!"

"Aw," groaned Pete. "I'm sleepy."

71

"But you have a job. The manager is depending on you to get the papers to the people. They should have them on time, too. Men like to read the morning paper before they go to work. Hurry!"

So Pete got up and delivered the pile of papers. But all his men customers were provoked. They had opened their doors, but not one of them had found a paper on his porch. When at last they heard the papers bang against the steps, it was too late to read them. They had to hurry off to work.

"You are a businessman, Pete," Daddy told him. "If you take pay, you must do your work well."

Pete was not so happy about his job now. It had seemed wonderful to know he would get ten dollars of his very own each month. He had dreamed about how he would spend the nine dollars after he had given one dollar to the Lord for a tithe. But it was hard work.

The next morning the alarm went off at six as usual. It was raining hard. Pete could hear the drops go drip, drip off the roof, and he just snuggled down in the warm bed and pulled the covers up around his ears.

When Mother discovered that Pete was still in bed, it was very late. No one on Pete's route got a paper at all that day.

That night Daddy read this Bible verse to Pete,

from a letter that Paul had written to the Christians at Rome: " 'Be . . . not slothful in business' (Romans 12:11)."

"*Slothful* means lazy," explained Daddy. "You belong to God. You say you want to please Him. You can't please Him by being lazy about your business."

"I want to quit," Pete grumbled.

"The manager is depending on you to deliver the papers every day and on time," said Daddy. "Ask God to help you do your job and do it right."

So Pete prayed.

"Help me, dear God, not to be a quitter. Help me not to be lazy. Help me to get up when the alarm rings and do my job right. In Jesus' Name. Amen."

They Find a Little Kitten

PETE RAN into the house.

"Where's the flashlight?" he asked. "I heard a kitten crying and I can't find it because it is dark."

"What were you doing outside in the dark?" Daddy wanted to know.

"I forgot to put my bike in the garage," answered Pete. "Come on, Daddy, help me find the kitten."

Penny put on her red jacket and hurried after Pete and Daddy.

"This way," Pete said. He flashed the light down the driveway. Where the light fell, they could see. On each side of the light, the darkness was black, and they could not see anything.

"Flash the light over here," Penny told Pete. "I think I hear a meow coming from this direction."

There it was again, a faint cry. Pete let the beam from the flashlight fall in front of him.

"Meow."

Crouched by a bush was a gray kitten. Its eyes were full of fright. It was about to run away, but it hesitated, and Pete grabbed hold of it.

He held it close and stroked its fur. He could feel its little heart beating wildly.

"Don't be afraid," he said.

Penny came close so she could pet the kitten, too.

"It is a good thing we had a flashlight," she said.

"We would have just stumbled around in the dark without it," agreed Pete.

Back in the house, Pete let Penny have a turn holding the frightened kitten. She sat on a stool by the fire and held it on her lap.

"That flashlight reminds me of the Bible," Daddy began. He opened his big Bible and read, " 'Thy word is a lamp unto my feet, and a light unto my path' (Psalm 119:105)."

"The flashlight," explained Daddy, "spread light on our path outdoors so we could see. Like a lamp that lights the way for our feet to walk in, the Bible, God's Word, shows us how to walk through life."

Penny nodded. Daddy was right.

"That is why," continued Daddy, "it is a good thing to read the Bible. It is better to memorize some of it." Then he turned to another place and read, " 'Thy word have I hid in mine heart, that I might not sin against thee' (Psalm 119:11)."

"How can learning a verse by heart keep us from sinning?" asked Pete.

"Well," said Mother, "suppose you'd go with a boy to the dime store and you'd see a little car you would like to have. It is marked 'ten cents' but you don't have ten cents. No one is looking. You might feel like sneaking that little car into your pocket and going home without paying for it. Then you would remember the verses from God's Word that say, 'Thou shalt not steal' (Exodus 20:15), and 'The eyes of the Lord are in every place, beholding the evil and the good' (Proverbs 15:3). Then what do you think you would do?"

"I would leave the little car alone and not steal it," Pete said.

"I want to learn lots of God's Word by heart," Penny said, as she rubbed her cheek on the kitten's soft fur. "It will help me not to sin against God."

A Vacant House

AFTER SCHOOL the next day, Pete did not play with Penny. He and Bob were playing catch with Bob's new ball in front of the house. Five boys from their classroom at school came by on their bikes.

"Hi, fellows!" the leader called. "Jump on your bikes and come along."

"Where are you going?" called Pete.

"We don't know. Just exploring."

"Come on," Bob coaxed. He jumped over the fence and disappeared. When he came back on his bike, Pete got on his and away they went.

"Remember what the state patrol sergeant said in assembly this morning," called Bob. "Boys on bikes should keep to the right, and use hand signals, just like drivers of cars."

The boy in front yelled, "OK I'll be the leader. You can all follow me and do what I do."

At the next corner he put his left arm straight out and turned to the left. All six boys following him did

the same thing. They rode two more blocks before he put his left arm out, bending it straight up at the elbow. Everyone knew they would be turning right.

"Follow the leader" was fun. On and on they rode until they came to a neighborhood Pete had never seen.

The leader stopped in front of a house and got off his bike. The rest did the same.

"What are we going to do?" Pete asked. "Does somebody know the people who live in this house?"

"Nobody lives in this house," one boy answered. "See? The shades are all pulled and there are papers on the porch." He picked up a stone.

"Let's see who can break the most windows with the fewest stones," he shouted. Then he threw a stone.

Crash! Glass splintered and shattered on to the porch.

"Hey!" protested Pete. "You can't do that!"

"Who says I can't? Watch me hit another." The boy stooped to pick up another stone. "Don't be a coward. It's fun. Try it!"

"I'm getting out of here," Pete mumbled. "Come on, Bob."

The two boys jumped on their bikes and rode toward home as fast as they could.

When Pete told Daddy about what had happened, Daddy opened his Bible and read:

> My son, if sinners entice thee, consent thou not . . . If they say, Come with us . . . My son, walk not thou in the way with them; refrain thy foot from their path (Proverbs 1:10-11, 15).

"*Entice* means to persuade," explained Daddy. "If bad boys try to persuade you to do wrong, like breaking windows, just get away from them as fast as you can. You and Bob did the right thing. *Consent thou not* means don't agree to help them do the wrong thing. Don't stay with them. If they get caught, even if you were only watching, you would be punished the same as they."

"I remembered the verse I learned by heart," said Pete. "Abhor that which is evil; cleave to that which is good" (Romans 12:9).

"That is why I came home as fast as I could."

A Surprise Visit

PETE AND PENNY were excited. Grandma Pendleton had come all the way from Oregon to visit for a few days. They would show her how pretty the mountains are in October, with the trees dressed in yellow and red.

"Come straight home from school," Mother told them. "Daddy will quit work at three o'clock. We will start soon after that."

"It takes an hour and a half to get to the mineral springs," Pete began. "Are we going to eat supper there?"

Already Mother was measuring sugar for a cake. "I shall have the food ready. We will surprise the Hunts. We can put our supper on the table with their supper, and we'll all eat together."

"I can't wait," Penny beamed. "I love that rushing river, and I want to ride one of the horses."

"Let's take some lemons and sugar and make lemon pop with the spring water," Pete said. "One spring tastes like soda water."

"This is going to be fun," Penny said as she kissed Mother good-by and started to school.

A little after three, the children burst in the door.

"Umm," said Penny. "It smells good in here. Roast beef? And look at the yummy cake. What else are we taking? Won't the Hunts be glad and surprised to have company for supper?"

"Where's Dad?" Pete asked. Just then, the phone rang. "I'll answer it."

80

Pete picked up the receiver.

"A little late? You can't leave when you planned to? OK I'll tell Mom."

Pete turned around. "Daddy will be late."

The children carried the boxes of food to the porch so that everything would be ready to load into the car the minute Daddy drove up. They sat on the steps and watched for him. Car after car went by, but not one was the light green car that belonged to the Pendletons.

Half an hour went by. A whole hour went by. An hour and a half went by.

Mother opened the door. "We can't go," she said. "Daddy can't get here."

"Can't go?" wailed Penny. "Mother, you don't mean it!"

"I do mean it. Maybe tomorrow. Bring the food in."

The family ate the delicious roast beef with vegetables and salad and finished with big wedges from the three-layer cake.

"We are the ones to be surprised," said Penny. "We are surprised to be eating at home." Then she pouted. "This is awful. I wanted to go. I don't see yet why we couldn't."

Daddy, who had just come home, opened his big Bible and read: " 'And we know that all things work together for good to them that love God' (Romans 8:28)."

"God had some reason," explained Daddy, "in not letting us go today. We don't know what it is, but we will believe that it was best for us not to go today."

Just then the doorbell rang. "Surprise!" called all the Hunts. "We came down from the mountain on business. We wanted to see you before we drove home."

While the Hunts ate cake, Pete and Penny knew that all things do work together for good to those who love God. How awful it would have been to have gone up the mountain, arriving at dark when the air was crisp, to discover the Hunt's door locked and no blazing fire to warm them. Yes, God knew best.

The Twins Learn to Be Satisfied

PETE AND PENNY were playing with their toys. Pete had his train tracks laid out on the floor, and he watched his little train chugging around and around.

But Pete wasn't happy. He kept thinking of Bob's train.

"Bob's train sure is nice," he said. "It's electric and

he has twice as much track as I have, and a tunnel and a bridge and a light that flashes off and on. I wish I had all these things. I wish Bob would give them to me."

"All of the Barber children's toys are nicer than ours," Penny complained. "Janey's doll is much bigger than this one of mine, and she has lots of pretty clothes for her doll. Janey's doll has hair that looks real. She can put curlers in it, even. I wish Janey's doll were my doll."

"Bob's bike is better than mine, too," Pete said. "It has big balloon tires and a push-button electric horn and twin headlights. I sure wish that bike was mine."

"And did you ever notice Janey's dresses?" asked Penny. "She had one on today I wish I had. It's red corduroy with fluffy white bunnies embroidered on the pockets. I wish—"

Daddy interrupted. He had come in with the corn-popper and some corn to pop. He was poking at the glowing coals in the fireplace.

"Do you know what *covet* means?" he asked.

Pete and Penny looked at each other.

"It is something you shouldn't do," Pete replied. "In the Ten Commandments in God's Word it says we shouldn't steal or kill or covet. But I don't know what *covet* means."

84

"To covet," said Daddy, "means to want something that belongs to somebody else."

"Just wishing for something isn't a sin," said Penny.

"God told us not to covet, and we had better not," replied Daddy. "If you want something your neighbor has, you might be tempted to steal it from him. And while you are stealing it, he might catch you and then there would be a fight. While you were fighting, you might hit him on the head so hard he would die. So," said Daddy, "let's not covet. Listen to this verse."

> Let your conversation be without covetousness; and be content with such things as ye have: for he hath said, I will never leave thee, nor forsake thee (Hebrews 13:5).

"Paul wrote this to some friends: 'I have learned, in whatsoever state I am, therewith to be content' (Philippians 4:11). It is a wonderful lesson to learn," added Daddy. Then he read:

> Every good gift and every perfect gift is from above, and cometh down from the Father of lights (James 1:17).

"I am glad," said Penny, "for the doll I have and for the dresses Mother makes for me and for the love at our house. I will be happy with what I have."

"Me, too," said Pete. "My bike is better than no bike, and it cost Daddy a lot of money." Then he prayed: "Dear God, help me to be content and happy with the good things You let me have. Help me not to covet other people's things. In Jesus' Name. Amen."

A Brand New House

MOVING DAY was a great day. It was the day that Pete and Penny Pendleton had been looking forward to for many months.

It had been exciting the day the bulldozer had chugged into the woods sending great trees crashing to the ground. A few weeks later, when the forms were ready, Pete and Penny had watched the cement trucks drive in and dump gooey grey concrete between the boards to make the basement walls and the foundation of the house.

Every night after work and on Saturdays, Daddy had gone over to saw boards and pound nails. The twins had helped, too, sometimes pulling nails from the forms, sometimes pounding nails or carrying boards. They had seen the walls go up and the roof go on. They had watched the windows and the doors go into place. They had seen holes drilled and wires poked through so they could have electric lights. They had watched the pipes being fitted so there would be water.

And at last they were moving from the tiny old house to a brand new house. It wasn't finished, really, because there was just a hole in the floor where the fireplace would be. And not all of the shiny hardwood floor had yet been laid over the rough floor boards.

But Pete and Penny would each have a room of their own. And there would be the woods around the house to play in. That's why they carried boxes and chairs off the truck and helped Daddy and his friends move beds and tables and dressers on moving day.

Penny helped Mother make the beds so that they would have a place to sleep. Because there wasn't time to cook, they had sandwiches and milk and cookies for supper. But they were eating in their new house. It was a great day!

Pete swallowed a bite of cheese sandwich. "We've been waiting for this day for an awful long time. It's almost too good to be true."

Penny nodded, and her brown curls bounced up and down. "I'm tired," she said, "but I'm happy. Just think! A brand new house to live in."

Mother smiled. "A new house is nice. We are

glad God gave us money to buy nails and boards and pipes and wire so that we could have this new house. But let's remember that we won't live here always."

Penny frowned. "We just moved in today and the house isn't even finished, really. Are you planning to move again?"

"I just want to remind us," answered Mother, "that God tells us about a heavenly home. We think that life will go on and on, but it won't." She got up, took Daddy's big Bible from a packing box, and read, " 'For we know that . . . we have a building of God, an house not made with hands, eternal in the heavens' (2 Corinthians 5:1)."

"This house was made with hands," Mother went on. "Of course Daddy had lots of tools, but his hands had to use them and tell them what to do. While we live on this earth we need a roof over our heads and a place to live. But we will not live on this earth forever. That house not made with hands, eternal in the heavens, is a house God has prepared for those who love Him."

"I'm going to live in it," said Pete.

"Are you sure?" Penny asked, and her brown eyes twinkled.

"Sure I'm sure," Pete told her. "Last summer when we were camping, I got to thinking about the bad things I'd done—my sins, you know. I knew *I* couldn't do anything to get rid of them. So I did what God tells us to do in His book. I believed that Jesus took the punishment for *my* sins. That was the day I became a child of God."

"And now you have eternal life," said Penny. "*Eternal* means you'll live forever and ever and ever, and you'll live in God's house in heaven because you belong to Him. I will, too, because I believe that Jesus died for me."

"We'll be happy in this house," said Daddy, "as long as God lets us live here, but we will be looking forward to the time when we can live in God's house, eternal in the heavens."

What Makes a Happy Home

IT TOOK A WEEK to get settled. Dishes had to be put into the cupboards, and a place had to be found for clothes, books, toys, and tools. There were lots of little jobs that Pete and Penny could do to help. When they weren't in school they ran errands and helped unpack.

"We haven't room for all the books here in the front room until the new bookshelves are made," said

Mother. "Here, Pete. Please take these books up-stairs."

Pete took the box upstairs, but it was a long time before he reported to Mother for another job. In answer to the questioning look on her face, he shrugged his shoulders.

"Just got to looking through some of the books," he said. "I get tired of work. I want to do what *I* want to do." There was a scowl on his face.

Penny was carrying a carton of muffin tins and baking pans from the front hall to the kitchen. She lost her grip.

"Pete," she yelped. "Help me a minute. *Please.*"

Pete strolled over.

"Hurry," panted Penny. "I can't hang on any longer."

"Then let 'er go," Pete shouted. Instead of lifting the corner of the carton that was slipping away from Penny, he knocked it with his knee so that she lost her hold completely. Baking pans clattered all over the front hall.

"You're horrid," Penny hissed. "You're no help at all." She knelt down and began to pick up pans. "You should pick some up. It's your fault."

"That's your job. I've got my own work to do," he grinned. He had been told to carry a bushel basket of fruit jars into the basement. He picked it up and scuttled down the stairs. Again he was gone a long time.

When Mother asked him what had kept him so long, he muttered, "I found my bag of marbles. Had to count my cat-eyes."

When Daddy came home, he heard a few reports.

"Pete's been bratty," Penny blamed her brother. Then she told about the spilled carton of baking pans.

Daddy observed some things during the evening. When the family gathered in the front room, just before the children's bedtime, he opened the Bible and read, " 'Behold, how good and how pleasant it is for brethren to dwell together in unity!' (Psalm 133:1)."

"We have a new house to live in," said Daddy, "but it will be just a house and not a home, if each person in the family doesn't decide to do his part in dwelling together in unity. We can live together under one roof, but we will be unhappy if we fight and bicker and quarrel. We must love one another. If we do that, we won't always be teasing and taunting one another. We will have unity. We will pull and work together. God says how good and pleasant that is."

Mother taught the family a new song. While Pete was repeating the words, he thought of the things he had done that day. Not all of them were kind. "We have a new house," said Pete. "We want it to be a happy home. I'll try to do my part."

Together they sang "God's Ways":

I'll make my home a happy home
By following God's ways;
If I am kind and loving there,
We shall have happy days.

I'll make my home a happy home
By following God's ways;
If I work well with others there,
We shall have happy days.

I'll make my home a happy home
By following God's ways;
If I don't ever quarrel there
We shall have happy days.*

Bricks and Mortar

THE FIRST BIG PROJECT of the Pendletons after they moved was building the fireplace. Everyone helped. Daddy measured the cement powder from a big bag into the wheelbarrow and added shovelfuls of lime and sand from the big barrel in the yard. Pete picked up the hoe and mixed the mortar. *Slop, slurp. Slop,*

Primaries Sing, published by Scripture Press.

slurp. It was like mixing mud pies, only Pete did not use his hands; he used a hoe. Daddy measured in some red powder so the mortar would match the bricks.

Penny and Mother carried bricks from the yard into the house, and when Pete had finished mixing the first batch of mortar, he carried bricks, too. With a big trowel, Daddy slapped mortar onto one brick and put it into place—then another and another. Pete picked up a smaller trowel and slapped mortar on the ends just as Daddy did. It was fun to press the hard red brick into the soft oozing mortar. Daddy had stretched a string across to keep the bricks in line. The rows of bricks must be straight and even.

"Now, while the mortar is soft," said Daddy, "we can put the bricks just where we want them. We can put them close together or far apart, crooked or straight. But the way we leave them when we go to bed tonight is the way they will always be. By morning the mortar will be hard as rock. If a brick is crooked, it will have to stay that way."

Pete stuck his tongue out of the corner of his mouth. He was trying hard to get his brick straight and even. "I don't want to be ashamed of my work," he said.

"There's a verse in the Bible I know," began Daddy, as he picked up a brick. " 'Whatsoever thy hand findeth to do, do it with thy might' (Ecclesiastes 9:10)."

"That means whatever your hands do, let them do the very best work they can." He quoted another verse. " 'Whatsoever ye do in word or deed, do all in the name of the Lord Jesus, giving thanks to God and the Father by Him' (Colossians 3:17)."

Penny had come with four more bricks just in time to hear what Daddy had said. She wrinkled her forehead. "If we invite someone to church, or give money to a missionary, we can do those things in the name of the Lord Jesus, but how can building a fireplace with bricks be done in His name?"

"Haven't you noticed how I use a square and measure when I'm building to get everything just right?" asked Daddy. "If the windowsills were crooked, and the chimney looked as if it were leaning, and my work were sloppy, the neighbors and friends we want to witness to about the goodness of God wouldn't feel like listening to us."

Mother spoke up. "I iron your dresses, Penny, and Pete's and Daddy's shirts the very best I can. I want you all to look neat and clean. I'm not preaching a sermon with my mouth while I do it, but I am doing the best work with my hands I can, in the Name of the Lord Jesus. If we all look neat on the outside, folks will feel more like listening to us when we want to talk to them about heavenly things."

"We can scrub floors or chop wood or lay bricks in a way that pleases God," said Daddy. "You notice it says, 'giving thanks to God and the Father by Him.' Happy hearts full of praise to God help our hands do good work."

Pete picked up a brick and slapped mortar on each end. He whistled a little tune. Penny recognized it, and the words of the song came to her as he whistled:

> Lord, I give thanks to Thee,
> Lord, I give thanks to Thee;
> Each lovely thing in this great world,
> Dear Lord, was made by Thee.*

And with a song in his heart and on his lips, Pete did the very best job he could with his hands.

Pete Strikes a Match

EACH EVENING Daddy and Pete mixed mortar and laid bricks until the fireplace was made, but they could not build a fire in it yet. They would have to build the chimney up through the hole in the upstairs floor and up through the roof. After school each day,

*Primaries Sing, published by Scripture Press.

Pete and Penny carried bricks upstairs and stacked them ready for Daddy to use. Brick by brick the chimney grew.

On a Friday afternoon late in October the job was finished. Pete stood on the platform Daddy had made on the roof and watched big yellow maple leaves, some streaked with red, flutter to the ground. The air felt nippy. Pete picked up the empty mortar bucket and carried it down the ladder. Daddy was beginning to scrub out the wheelbarrow for the last time.

Pete blew onto his fingers to warm them and stamped his feet. "A fire will sure feel good tonight," he said.

"Guess we'll have to wait until this time tomorrow," Daddy told him. "If we build a fire before the cement is hard, it will crumble and break."

But Pete crumpled up paper and laid kindling on it and filled the woodbasket with logs so that they would be ready when Daddy asked him to light a fire.

It was late Saturday afternoon when Daddy said he supposed a very small fire would not hurt the mortar in the chimney. Daddy nodded when Pete asked for permission to strike the match. He and Penny both knew that they were never to strike a match unless Daddy or Mother was there to watch.

Pete lighted the fire. All four in the family were

happy when they saw the smoke drift up the chimney. Sometimes chimneys are not made right and the smoke fills the room. But their fireplace and chimney really worked.

"I've always taken a fireplace for granted," said Mother. "Nearly every house we walk into has a fireplace. Of course, I knew it was work to make them. But I never realized how much."

Pete nodded. He knew what she meant. He sat on the floor and hugged his knees while he stared at the fire and felt its friendly warmth on his body. He was quiet for a long time. Finally he said, "There's a new kid up the street. Mike's his name. I told him I couldn't decide which I liked best of the four seasons God has made. Winter is nice when you can go sledding in the snow, and spring is exciting when the new leaves come on the trees such a pretty bright green, and of course I like to swim and hike in summer, but there's something nice about the nippy days in fall and it's fun to crunch the dry leaves beneath a fellow's feet."

"Which season did Mike say he liked?" asked Daddy.

"Aw, he never told me. Just said, 'Who's God? There isn't any God. My Dad said so.' I asked him who he thought made the world and everything in it. He said he guessed the world just happened."

Pete looked up at the bricks that stretched to the ceiling. "First chance I get, I'm bringing him over to look at this fireplace. I'll ask him if he thinks the bricks just happened to fall into place by themselves."

Penny broke in. "He will have to believe you when you tell him you and Daddy smeared mortar on each brick and stone and laid them in place."

"It's the same with a watch or a house or a dress or most anything," Pete went on. "Somebody had to plan them and somebody had to make them. They didn't just happen to fall together. Only we use materials God has already provided. God just spoke and the world was made in the first place."

Daddy was sitting in the rocking chair by the fire. He was thumbing through his Bible. "Here is a verse you can show your friend Mike."

> Thus saith the Lord. . . . I have made the earth, and created man upon it: I, even my hands, have stretched out the heavens, and all their host have I commanded (Isaiah 45:11-12).

Pete Earns a Bible

PETE COULD HEAR the raindrops pattering on the roof overhead. He snuggled down into bed and pulled

100

the blankets tighter around his neck. It would be a perfect morning to lie in bed, listen to the rain, and think. Then the tune of the song, "I love to tell the story of Jesus and His love," came drifting up from the kitchen just below. That was the theme song for the Family Bible Hour heard on the radio every Sunday morning. It was Pete's signal that it was time to get up.

If Mother didn't hear Pete stirring very soon, she would call up the stairs. If she had to call more than once before he got up, she would be unhappy. He wasn't supposed to be late for breakfast, and Daddy would not like it if Pete ran to the table without his shoes on or his hair combed or his necktie straight. If he had to gobble his breakfast rolls and gulp his milk so he wouldn't be late to Sunday school, the day would have a bad start. No, it would be better to get up and have time to dress, to eat, and to get to Sunday school on time.

Pete stretched one last time before he hopped out of bed. He really wanted to go to Sunday school today, too. Of course he went every Sunday. Mother and Daddy and Penny and he always went, but today was going to be very special for two reasons. If Pete could recite the One Hundredth Psalm perfectly he would receive a Bible of his own. And Daddy had said that Pete could take his great-grandfather's sword to Sunday school to show everyone.

Pete dressed in a hurry. He could when he wanted to, Mother always told him, only lots of times he just wanted to poke.

While the family ate, Pete said the One Hundredth Psalm, so as to be sure he still knew it perfectly.

When it was time to leave, Pete proudly carried the big heavy sword in its brass and leather case.

At Sunday school, during the worship service, Mr. Scott, the superintendent, asked Pete if he was ready to recite his Psalm.

Pete stood in front of the group. He cleared his throat. Then he said:

> "Make a joyful noise unto the LORD, all ye lands. Serve the LORD with gladness: come before his presence with singing. Know ye that the LORD he is God: it is he that hath made us, and not we ourselves; we are his people, and the sheep of his pasture. Enter into his gates with thanksgiving, and into his courts with praise: be thankful unto him, and bless his name. For the LORD is good; his mercy is everlasting, and his truth endureth to all generations."

The boys and girls had listened quietly. Mr. Scott had followed along in his Bible.

"Perfect," he exclaimed. "You didn't have to be prompted once and you made no mistakes. I am

103

happy to present this Bible to you on behalf of our Sunday school."

Pete accepted the big box. "Thanks," he said. "Thanks a lot."

At last he had a Bible of his own. He had carried a little New Testament to Sunday school since he was small. Lately Mother had loaned him her old Bible. But Pete had wanted a Bible of his own. And now he had one. He had earned a copy of God's Word. It was his. Pete grinned.

It's Real to Pete and Penny

PETE STRETCHED wire across the front of his rabbit hutch and stapled it on.

"A fellow at school promised me a rabbit as soon as I get a place to keep it," he told Penny.

Penny already knew that. She nodded. "That's a real nice rabbit hutch," she said. "I can't wait until we get our bunny rabbit."

"What do you mean 'our' rabbit?" demanded Pete. "This whole thing was my idea."

Penny looked hurt. "You'll let me take turns feeding it, and I can play with it, too, can't I, Pete? Please," pleaded Penny.

"Well, maybe," Pete said. He was screwing a hinge to the door. "But if you get to feed it and play with it, you'll have to take turns cleaning the hutch. That's only fair."

"OK," agreed Penny.

That night Pete and Penny had fun watching the rabbit hop around in the front room. Penny held it on her lap and stroked its long ears. They were soft as silk. She liked to watch it wrinkle its nose and twitch its whiskers. Pete asked Mother for a carrot, and Penny held it while the rabbit chewed off a piece.

"What's her name?" asked Penny. "Let's call her Sweetie Pie."

"That's no name for a rabbit. I guess I'll call her Hinkabus. Hinky for short."

Penny stroked the rabbit's soft white fur. "Poor bunny. How can you be happy with a name like that?" Then she let her hop on the floor. "I hope nothing happens to Hinky. I hope she doesn't die like our first little chicks did. It's so sad when a pet dies."

"Yeh," agreed Pete. "Still, there's lots more rabbits in the world. We could easily get another one. But when a person that you know dies, that's sad. If Mother or Daddy died, or you, I'd feel pretty bad."

"But we believe in the resurrection, you know," Penny said. "Even if somebody we love dies and we are sad, we know we will see them again. That's if they were saved by believing in Jesus before they died."

Daddy came in to sit by the fire just in time to hear what Penny said.

"I'm glad to hear that the resurrection is real to my children," he smiled. "Lots of folks who were alive when Jesus died and rose again would not believe that He really came alive again. There are still plenty of people who refuse to believe it."

Pete said, "You know how come I believe? Well, when the angel told those women that Jesus was alive, they ran and told Peter and John. They both dashed to the sepulchre—that's the cave where they had put Jesus' body, you know. Well, what they saw made them believe." Daddy had been glancing through the Bible he had picked up from the lamp table. "Here," he said, "let me read this:"

> Then cometh Simon Peter following him, and went into the sepulchre, and seeth the linen clothes lie, And the napkin, that was about his head, not lying with the linen clothes, but wrapped together in a place by itself. Then went in also that other disciple, which came first to the sepulchre, and he saw, and believed (John 20:6-8).

Penny spoke up. "Sure. I believe Jesus came alive. If somebody had stolen the body, the linen clothes they had wrapped around His body would have been

106

crumpled up in a corner or not there at all. But there they were, all wrapped neatly together and the napkin that had been on his head, lying just where it had been when he slipped out of his grave clothes."

"And the fact that Jesus rose from the dead means we will, too," added Daddy. He had turned to another place in the Bible and continued reading, " 'But now is Christ risen from the dead, and become the firstfruits of them that slept' (1 Corinthians 15:20)." "The first ripe strawberry tells us that soon there will be a crop of strawberries. The fact that Christ arose, means we can be sure that even if we die, someday we will rise from the dead."

"Just think, we are going to live forever. Even if we die, we'll come alive again. Then we'll have nice new bodies that won't get sick, either." Then Pete gathered Hinky into his arms and took her outside to her new hutch.

The Golden Text for Penny

PENNY SNEAKED in the back door, but it squeaked like it always did.

"Is that you, Penny?" called Mother from the sewing room. "What have you been doing?"

Penny laid a bow and two arrows on the kitchen table as quietly as she could. "Oh, nothing," she answered.

"Come here," Mother called. When Penny poked her face in the door, she said, "Now, Penny, what *were* you doing?"

"Well," answered Penny. "I was shooting arrows with Pete's bow."

Mother was hemming a dress and her eyes were on the needle. "How nice of Pete to share his bow and arrows," she said. "He saved up a long time to buy them, and he's very proud of them. He's so careful I was afraid he wouldn't be willing to share them. That was nice of him."

Penny was glad that Mother was looking at her sewing.

"Well, er—Pete doesn't exactly know he shared," she said in a very small voice.

Mother looked up quickly with surprise in her eyes. "You mean you just helped yourself to the bow and arrows and used them without Pete's permission?"

Penny traced the pattern in the rug with the toe of her shoe. She nodded her head. "Pete wasn't around," she said lamely, "so I couldn't ask him." Penny wished Mother wouldn't look at her that way. "I—I shot an arrow into the woods and—and—and now I can't find it."

Mother looked very unhappy. "You borrowed Pete's bow and arrows without asking? And now you've lost an arrow so you can't give it back!"

Penny wished she could sink through a hole and disappear.

"Your roller skates are most important to you," Mother said. "How would you like it if Pete just took them without asking you and threw them back in your closet with one wheel missing? How would you—"

Penny's brown eyes flashed. "Pete wouldn't dare. He knows I spent my story check on those skates and had to save a lot of allowances besides. He just wouldn't dare!" Her voice was loud and she stamped her foot.

"*You* dared—and *you* did," said Mother quietly. "And yesterday when I decided to wear my red flower on my white blouse I discovered a little girl had helped herself to it and had worn it in her hair all day. When Daddy was tired last Saturday, from gardening, he decided to put up the hammock, but he couldn't. Do you know why?"

Penny looked down at the floor. "I needed a new jumping rope so I—"

"—helped myself to the hammock rope," Mother

finished for her. Then Mother reached for a Bible and read:

> Let nothing be done through strife or vainglory; but in lowliness of mind let each esteem other better than themselves. Look not every man on his own things, but every man also on the things of others (Philippians 2:3-4).

"I'm afraid," Mother said, "that a little girl named Penelope Elaine Pendleton has been fixing attention on her own interests. Whatever Penny wants, she takes. She doesn't care who it belongs to or how much it means to them. She just helps herself. If she had fixed her attention on the interests of others, she would have asked Pete's permission for the use of his bow and arrows. Yesterday, she would have said to herself, 'I would love Mother's red flower to wear in my hair, but maybe she is planning to use it. I'll ask.' On Saturday, when she wanted a jump rope, she would have asked Daddy to find her a piece of rope that wasn't in use, instead of ruining the hammock. I think this little girl needs to say the golden text over to herself. That's a Bible verse that will help her do right."

Penny said softly,

> And as ye would that men should do to you, do ye also to them likewise (Luke 6:31).

111

Then she turned and went outside. She would have to find that lost arrow or buy another one. And after this, with God's help, she would think about the interests of others.

Marriage Is for Keeps

PENNY WAS PROUD of her pretty pink dress. There were little blue bows sprinkled all over the full skirt and she had new blue gloves, the same shade of blue as the bows on her skirt.

"Hurry, Pete," she called as she pulled on a glove. "Mother and Daddy are ready to go." Pete bounded down the stairs. "Isn't it exciting, Pete? We've never been to a wedding before."

The Pendletons found places in the balcony at the church so the children could see everything.

Penny sat on the edge of the seat and looked.

"The flowers—" she whispered. "Mother, aren't the flowers beautiful? There are six huge baskets full of pink and white flowers."

The organ music was soft and beautiful. Two girls in pretty dresses lighted dozens and dozens of candles.

Gradually the music grew louder and the people

who were in the wedding party started to come in. One by one, they came, walking slowly and gracefully. The men were dressed in their best suits and the young ladies, wearing long full dresses of pale pink and deep pink, carried bouquets of white flowers tied with shiny satin ribbons. They took their places in the front of the church. Then everyone in the church stood up. The bride was coming!

Penny thought that the bride was beautiful in her long white dress and flowing veil. She carried pink and white flowers.

"Do you take this woman to be your wedded wife?" Penny heard the preacher ask.

Penny couldn't hear the answer, but she knew the groom said, "I do." That was the man the pretty bride was marrying.

She listened while they each promised to love and take care of the other through their whole lives. They gave each other a ring to prove that they meant what they said.

Soon the preacher said, "I pronounce you man and wife," and then the groom kissed the bride. Both of them had big smiles on their faces as they turned and walked to the back of the church.

At the reception, Penny watched the bride cut the cake that looked like a tall tower, all yummy with pink and white frosting. Everyone was laughing and happy. A wedding was really exciting.

On the way home, Penny said, "I can't wait to get married. I think it would be fun to be the bride and have flowers and presents."

"I hope," said Mother, "that you will wait until you find the right man."

Pete piped up from the back seat. "I want to find the right girl, too. But how are we supposed to know which one is the right one? Did you notice? The bride and groom each promised to love and take care of the other one until they die. That's a long time. That's the rest of their lives. Getting married is for keeps. How are Penny and I supposed to know who are the right ones for us to marry?"

Daddy slowed down for a stop sign. "The Bible is the best guide," he said.

"How can the Bible help?" asked Penny. "It doesn't say, 'Penny, you marry Mike.' How can I know whom to marry?"

"The Bible gives us some good rules to go by," explained Mother. Then she quoted a verse:

> Be ye not unequally yoked together with unbelievers: for what fellowship hath righteousness with unrighteousness? And what communion hath light with darkness? (2 Corinthians 6:14).

"You know what a yoke is?" interrupted Daddy. "It's a big wooden collar that was used to put on the necks of two oxen so they could pull a wagon together, or plough together. If an ox would be yoked with a horse, what would happen?"

Pete knew. "The horse would go lots faster than the old ox. They wouldn't pull together. Nobody should yoke them together in the first place."

"Right," said Daddy. "God is telling us that believers and unbelievers should not be yoked together in marriage. You love the Lord Jesus Christ, Pete. You have taken Him as your Saviour. Be very sure that the girl you marry loves Him, too."

"There's a girl in our Sunday school class," said Penny. "Her father is saved, but her mother isn't. Betty is at Sunday school only half the time. Her dad likes her to go, but her mother is always planning picnics and trips so she can't be there."

"The important thing is to find the *right* Christian for you. You need to love each other, of course. No one is perfect. You will have to love that person enough to be married to her the rest of your life, in spite of her faults."

"And you should enjoy doing the same things," Mother added. "Deciding whom to marry is a very important matter. Each of you will have to ask the Lord to help you know."

"That bride sure was pretty," said Penny, "and I want to be one, but not until God shows me the very person He wants me to marry. God will help me know when the time comes. I know He will."

Red Ring on the Calendar

ONE DAY Hinkabus began to pull fur from her breast with her mouth. Soon the box in her rabbit hutch was full of fluff.

"What's she doing that for?" Penny asked her father. "That shredded newspaper in the box makes a pretty soft nest."

"But baby bunnies are naked little things," Father answered. "God teaches the mother rabbit to wrap her tiny babies in bits of fur pulled from her own body until they grow their own coats of fur. Some folks would say that 'mother nature' teaches them, but I have never figured out who they mean by 'mother nature.' It is God who teaches the mother rabbit to prepare for the babies that will soon be born."

Although the red ring on the calendar told Pete and Penny that the babies would not be born for four more days, the children anxiously watched. And even on the right day, Hinkabus sat in her box and neither Pete nor Penny could tell if there were babies in the nest or not. When Pete reached his hand into the hutch to stroke Hinkabus, she bit him.

"Why, Hinky!" exclaimed Pete. "You never did that before."

Suspicious, Pete finally lured Hinkabus to the other side of the hutch with a carrot. While the rabbit nibbled, Penny lifted the lid to the box where her nest was.

"Don't put your hand in the nest," Pete warned. "If there are babies and you touch them, Hinky will be able to tell by the smell and she might kill them."

Pete went around the box where he could see better. "Say," he exclaimed, "that fluff is moving! Look, Penny. Aren't those babies?"

"Pete! They *are* baby bunnies. Only they aren't cute. They look like pigs. Oh, Pete. I thought a baby bunny looked just like a big bunny, only smaller."

"Give them time," Pete told Penny. "It won't be long before they grow fur and look real cute. You'll see."

"But what can we feed them?" Penny wondered.

"You and Pete don't have to worry about that." Mother had come to see the new family. "Hinkabus will feed her babies."

"How can she do that?"

118

"Why on her underneath side are a lot of little nipples. Each little bunny just needs to nuzzle around until he finds one and suck on it. That milk was made for baby bunnies. They'll grow and be cute in no time."

Penny was puzzled. When they were back in the house she asked, "Where does Hinky's milk come from? Does she have some all the time?"

Mother was peeling potatoes. "No," she answered. "Having milk is part of this business of having babies. There are glands that fill with milk as soon as the babies are born and need food."

"I can't figure it out," Penny said. "No babies, no milk. Then the babies are born and there's milk. It's almost like magic."

"Not magic, Penny. God is great and wise and powerful. He made rabbits in the first place. He planned so baby rabbits would grow inside the mother and be born. He planned so that the helpless little things would have milk to drink until they are big enough to eat grass and cabbage and carrots. When we think how God planned and worked out every detail it makes us realize how wonderful He is. 'O Lord, thou art my God; I will exalt thee, I will praise thy name; for thou hast done wonderful things' (Isaiah 25:1)."

119

The House Is Finished

WHEN THE TINY BUNNIES had fur and were big enough to play with, Pete and Penny spent many hours holding them and stroking their soft fur. They liked to watch them hop around and wrinkle up their noses when they ate grass, just like their mother did.

It was after supper. Mother was pulling weeds from among the pansy plants and Daddy was putting up the last pieces of siding on the house.

"I will be ready to start painting the house next week," he said. "A chocolate brown color with green trim around the windows will look mighty nice."

Penny counted the bunnies to see if they were all there. Yes, seven little white rabbits were snuggling around Hinkabus. Penny took one from the hutch and held it to her cheek. She liked the soft warmth of the fur on her face.

"Daddy," she began, "the preacher said Sunday that Jesus might come back any day. Perhaps today. Why bother to finish the house? When Jesus comes back, all the people who have taken Him as their own Saviour will rise right up in the air and meet Him in the sky. Then we will live with Him for ever and ever. I know. You read all about it to us from the

Bible. After Jesus comes, we won't need this house any more. So why finish it?"

Daddy was on a ladder. He had nails in his mouth. He pounded them into the cedar siding before he answered.

"True," he said. "Jesus is coming back and we are to be watching and waiting." He quoted a Bible verse that says:

> For our conversation is in heaven; from whence also we look for the Saviour, the Lord Jesus Christ; who shall change our vile body, that it might be fashioned like unto his glorious body (Philippians 3:20-21).

Pete piped up. "God is happy when we talk about wanting Jesus to come back, isn't He, Daddy? And just think. You won't have a stiff back any more. And those two fingers that don't work so good will be perfect again."

"We're to look for Him, that's for sure," said Mother. She tossed another handful of weeds into the pile. Then she recited one of her favorite verses:

> So Christ was once offered to bear the sins of many; and unto them that look for him shall he appear the second time without sin unto salvation (Hebrews 9:28).

"But just folding your hands and waiting isn't the way to look for Him, is it Daddy?" Pete asked. "We

121

are supposed to ask the Lord to show us His will and His plan for our lives and then work as hard as we can at it. Mother went to the store one afternoon and when she came home and found out Penny had just been killing time instead of setting the table and practicing the piano, she wasn't very happy. While we are waiting for Jesus to come back, we should be busy, shouldn't we?"

Daddy was back up on the ladder with another board. He knew another Bible verse:

> And now, little children, abide in him; that, when he shall appear, we may have confidence, and not be ashamed before him at his coming (1 John 2:28).

Penny put the baby bunny back with Hinkabus. "I guess we better finish the house," she said. "And I'll help mother keep it neat and clean. We don't want to be ashamed when Jesus comes. He wouldn't like it if He found us being lazy."

"He wouldn't like it, either," said Mother, "if He found us so busy fixing the house and yard, and cooking and sewing we never had time to go to church or read the Bible or tell other people about Him. There's a happy balance. We can want Jesus to come back and we can look for Him and expect Him, but we can be busy and happy while we wait."

Hand in Hand with Jesus

PENNY WAS LICKING the fudge pan. When Pete came in the kitchen door and saw what she was doing, he hurried and got himself a big spoon and was going to do some scraping, too. Penny was tempted to pull the pan away from him saying, "Get out of here. Mother said *I* could lick this fudge pan." Then she remembered that if Pete had been there first, she would have wanted *him* to share with her. So they scraped and licked together.

"Mother," Penny said, "if I could just *see* God I'd be happy. It's sort of hard to love somebody you've never seen."

"Nobody has ever seen God," Mother replied, and she quoted a verse:

> No man hath seen God at any time; the only begotten Son, which is in the bosom of the Father, he hath declared him (John 1:18).

"When Jesus was on earth He told us and showed us what God is like," Mother continued as she cut the fudge into squares and piled them on a plate. She passed it to Penny and then to Pete. "It's not hard to love someone who loves you. All the good gifts God has given us remind us of His great love. Why,

123

even a drink of cold water is proof of His love. Every bright little flower, our food, the rain, the sun, nighttime to sleep, and the very air we breathe are all gifts from God."

"Well, anyway, if I just could have lived on earth when Jesus was here so I could have seen Him with my own eyes, I'd be happier," said Penny, licking her lips to get every crumb of that good candy.

"After Jesus died and rose again," said Mother, "He gave His disciples final instructions, and then a promise."

> Go ye therefore, and teach all nations . . .Teaching them to observe all things whatsoever I have commanded you; and lo, I am with you alway, even unto the end of the world (Matthew 28:19-20).

"Right this minute Jesus is in heaven, but He is also here, because of that promise to be with us always."

Pete knew a song about that. He went to the piano and picked out the tune with one finger and sang as he played:

> "I am with you always," Jesus says to me.
> Though His face I cannot see,
> Still beside me He will be;
> In His Word He says to me:
> "Lo! I am with you, Lo! I am with you,
> Lo! I am with you always."*

*Primaries Sing, published by Scripture Press.

Penny decided she would remember that Jesus was with her always. Lots of times she had said things and thought things and done things that she would have been ashamed for Jesus to know about. And yet He did know about them. No one can hide from God, and Jesus is God. Then, too, if she remembered that Jesus was with her always, she would not be afraid in the dark or to give the mailman a story-tract about needing to be friends with God. She would play fair and do her work cheerfully and well. She would not pout nor cry when she was disappointed. There were lots of things she would do differently if she remembered that Jesus was with her always.

Penny talked this over with Pete.

"Yes," agreed Pete, "you and I will be happier in our hearts, and our home will be happier and the world, even, if we walk hand in hand with the Lord Jesus Christ. And we will grow as we know Him better."

Penny found herself humming a song. Pete recognized it.

"That's a good song," said Pete. "It's a good prayer song to sing at the start of each day."

Pete and Penny opened their mouths and together they sang:

126

Dear Jesus, walk with me,
Walk with me today—
Work with me, play with me,
Show me what is Thy best way—
Dear Jesus, walk with me,
Walk with me today.

Dear Jesus, I need Thee,
Close to Thee I'll stay—
I love Thee, I trust Thee,
I'll obey Thee every day—
Dear Jesus, I need Thee,
Close to Thee I'll stay.*

*_Primaries Sing_, published by Scripture Press.

WITHDRAWN